AF419744

Rising in Radiance
Embrace Your Divine Journey

BELONGS TO

____

DATE

____

Embrace Your Divine Journey

Dedication

To every radiant Black woman who graces the pages of this journal:

May your journey through these pages be as profound as the legacy of strength, grace, and resilience that courses through your veins. Let each word you pen be a testament to your divine purpose, an affirmation of your immeasurable worth, and a beacon of hope for the dreams yet to unfold. In a world that may sometimes cast shadows upon your brilliance, may this journal serve as a sanctuary, a place where your spirit is celebrated, your voice is amplified, and your connection to the Almighty is fortified.

With every reflection, every prayer, and every revelation, know that you are not just writing for yourself but for the generations of Black women who came before and those yet to come. You are the embodiment of grace, a vessel of divine love, and the keeper of an eternal flame. Here is to your spiritual voyage, one that will undoubtedly leave an indelible mark on the annals of time.

Dive deep, rise high, and let your spirit soar!

Embrace Your Divine Journey

Introduction

Welcome, radiant soul, to a journey of profound depth, spiritual enlightenment, and personal discovery. *Rising Radiance: Embrace Your Divine Journey* isn't just a journal; it's an intimate dialogue with your innermost self, a sacred space where your spirit is free to express, explore, and expand. Before you begin, understand that there is no right or wrong way to engage with these pages. They are yours to fill, a canvas for your thoughts, prayers, and reflections. Why *Rising Radiance?*

Because your journey is a testament to the power that dwells within a life lived in conversation with God. As a black woman, your narrative is rich with history and hope, a unique blend of past, present, and future, all deserving of acknowledgment, celebration, and divine communion.

In *Rising Radiance*, you will find a platform to voice your innermost yearnings, a wellspring of inspiration for those moments when you need it most, and a mirror reflecting your own divine light. This journal stands as a reminder that your prayers are powerful, your faith is formidable, and your story is continuously unfolding in the most beautiful and mystical of ways.

Accept this invitation to etch your journey within these pages and let *Rising Radiance* be your guide and confidant as you embrace the divine journey that is uniquely, incredibly yours. Rise in your radiance, for every page turned is a new horizon of hope, strength, and divine connection.

Begin your journey, own your narrative, and let *Rising Radiance* accompany you every step of the way. Your divine journey awaits. Here's how you can make the most of your journey.

Before you pen your first entry, pause, and breathe deeply. Reflect on your intention for this journey. Are you seeking growth, healing, clarity, or perhaps, a deeper connection with The Lord? Whatever it is, write it down. Let it be the guiding light of your journey through this journal.

Dedicate a specific time and place for your journaling practice. Early mornings as the sun rises or quiet evenings can be ideal for introspection. Ensure this space is free from distractions, allowing you to fully connect with your thoughts and emotions. Each prompt is designed to guide you deeper into your soul's landscape. Don't just skim the surface; use them as a diving board into the depths of your experiences, dreams, and spiritual insights. Let honesty be your compass, and vulnerability, your strength.

Accompanying scriptures are woven into the journal, providing divine wisdom and guidance. Reflect on them, letting the words simmer in your mind How do they resonate with your life? Are there personal revelations or interpretations you feel compelled to explore?

Allow your prayers to flow freely onto the pages. They can be words of gratitude, requests for strength, or petitions for guidance. Visualize your prayers ascending, knowing they're heard and held by The Lord.

After writing, take a moment to pause and sit in silence. Meditate on the insights revealed, the emotions evoked, and the spiritual guidance received. How do they shape your understanding of yourself and your journey?

Periodically revisit previous entries. Witnessing your spiritual evolution over time can be a powerful experience. Celebrate your growth, acknowledge your struggles, and marvel at the never-ending journey of self-discovery.

Conclude each session with a note of thanks. Express gratitude for the wisdom unveiled, the emotional release, and the divine connection experienced. Gratitude is, after all, the heart's memory.

"...Whatever you ask in prayer, believe that you have received it, and it will be yours." Mark 11:24

Promise to Pray

Your *Promise to Pray* is a commitment to growth. With each prayer, you develop spiritually, emotionally, and mentally. It's an acknowledgment that this practice will shape you in profound ways, drawing you ever closer to the woman you're destined to be.

As you embark on this sacred commitment, know that prayer is more than a ritual; it is a lifestyle. The pages ahead are ready to bear witness to your journey, and in them, you will find not just words, but the very echoes of your soul's evolution.

By making this promise, you commit to setting aside sacred moments each day exclusively for prayer. It is about prioritizing your spiritual nourishment and forging a habit that anchors your day in gratitude, reflection, and divine connection.

Prayer transcends mere recitation; it is a dialogue with The Lord. Your promise is to engage authentically, bringing your true self into this sacred space, bearing your hopes, fears, dreams, and gratitude. It is about being present, open, and honest, ready to both speak and listen to God. Your intercession is a powerful act of love and solidarity.

Life has its seasons, and your promise is to remain steadfast in prayer through each one. Whether in times of joy or periods of struggle, your commitment is to turn to prayer as your constant, knowing it is a source of strength, guidance, and comfort. Preparing your heart to receive what's for you, not the expectation of how. Sometimes, prayers are answered in unexpected ways. By committing to pray, you declare that you're ready to embrace the responses, lessons, and blessings that come, however they may appear.

Post-prayer reflection is vital. You commit to pondering your prayer experiences, noting how they affect you, and discerning any divine insights. This journal will serve as a repository for these reflections, helping you track your spiritual evolution.

Promise to pray, promise to trust, promise to grow. The journey awaits!

Embrace Your Divine Journey

SPIRITUAL GOALS

How will I spend time with God?

How will I serve others?

Which fruits of the spirit will I work on?

What Bible verse will I remember?

Rising in Radiance

Scriptures are reminders that no matter the journey, you are never alone, for your steps are ordered by the Lord.
Embrace these truths and let them anchor your soul!

Go to Scriptures

Proverbs 31:25
She is clothed with strength and dignity, and she laughs without fear of the future.

Joshua 1:9
Have I not commanded you? Be strong and courageous. Do not be afraid; do not be discouraged, for the Lord your God will be with you wherever you go.

Psalm 46:5
God is within her, she will not fall; God will help her at break of day.

Luke 1:45
Blessed is she who has believed that the Lord would fulfill his promises to her!

Proverbs 31:30
Charm is deceptive, and beauty is fleeting; but a woman who fears the Lord is to be praised.

I Corinthians 15:10
But by the grace of God, I am what I am, and his grace to me was not without effect. No, I worked harder than all of them — yet not I, but the grace of God that was with me.

Philippians 4:13
I can do all things through Christ who strengthens me.

II Timothy 1:7
For God has not given us a spirit of fear, but of power and of love and of a sound mind.

Jeremiah 29:11
For I know the plans I have for you, declares the Lord, plans to prosper you and not to harm you, plans to give you hope and a future.

Proverbs 11:16
A kindhearted woman gains honor, but ruthless men gain only wealth.

II Timothy 1:7
For God has not given us a spirit of fear, but of power and of love and of a sound mind.

Matthew 5:16
In the same way, let your light shine before others, that they may see your good deeds and glorify your Father in heaven.

John 16:33
I have told you these things, so that in me you may have peace. In this world you will have trouble. But take heart! I have overcome the world.

Psalm 20:4
May he give you the desire of your heart and make all your plans succeed.

Romans 12:12
Be joyful in hope, patient in affliction, faithful in prayer.

Ephesians 2:10
For we are God's handiwork, created in Christ Jesus to do good works, which God prepared in advance for us to do.

Embrace Your Divine Journey

Deuteronomy 31:6
*Be strong and
courageous. Do not be
afraid or terrified
because of them, for
the Lord your God
goes with you; he will
never leave you nor
forsake you.*

I Peter 2:9
*But you are a chosen
people, a royal
priesthood, a holy
nation, God's special
possession, that you
may declare the
praises of him who
called you out of
darkness into his
wonderful light.*

Romans 8:28
*And we know that in
all things God works
for the good of those
who love him, who
have been called
according to his
purpose.*

Micah 6:8
*He has shown you, O
mortal, what is good.
And what does the
Lord require of you?
To act justly and to
love mercy and to
walk humbly with
your God.*

Hebrews 10:35-36
*So do not throw away
your confidence; it
will be richly
rewarded. You need
to persevere so that
when you have done
the will of God, you
will receive what he
has promised.*

Isaiah 40:31
*But those who hope in
the Lord will renew
their strength. They
will soar on wings
like eagles; they will
run and not grow
weary, they will walk
and not faint.*

Rising in Radiance

Proverbs 3:15-18
*She is more precious
than rubies; nothing
you desire can
compare with her.
Long life is in her
right hand; in her left
hand are riches and
honor. Her ways are
pleasant ways, and all
her paths are peace.
She is a tree of life to
those who take hold of
her; those who hold
her fast will be
blessed.*

Isaiah 41:10
*So do not fear, for I
am with you; do not
be dismayed, for I am
your God. I will
strengthen you and
help you; I will
uphold you with my
righteous right hand.*

Esther 4:14
*Perhaps you were
born for such a time
as this.*

I Peter 3:3-4
*Your beauty should
not come from
outward adornment,
such as elaborate
hairstyles and the
wearing of gold
jewelry or fine
clothes. Rather, it
should be that of your
inner self, the
unfading beauty of a
gentle and quiet
spirit, which is of
great worth in God's
sight.*

Philippians 4:6-7
*Do not be anxious
about anything, but
in every situation, by
prayer and petition,
with thanksgiving,
present your requests
to God. And the peace
of God, which
transcends all
understanding, will
guard your hearts and
your minds in Christ
Jesus.*

Embrace Your Divine Journey

I am believing in God for...

- ☐ ____
- ☐ ____
- ☐ ____
- ☐ ____
- ☐ ____
- ☐ ____
- ☐ ____
- ☐ ____
- ☐ ____
- ☐ ____
- ☐ ____
- ☐ ____
- ☐ ____
- ☐ ____
- ☐ ____
- ☐ ____

"*Your spirit is an unbreakable force, resilient and enduring. Stand firm in your convictions, for within you lies an ocean of strength, ready to rise against any tide.*"

Embrace Your Divine Journey

5 Minute Blessing Journal

__/__/___

S M T W TH F S

Breathe before writing

INHALE EXHALE INHALE EXHALE INHALE EXHALE

How God blessed me today:

What song is in your heart?

3 blessings I received today:

Today's Highlight

Things that I learned today

Today's Scripture

Identity in Christ

Psalm 139:14 - I praise you because I am fearfully and wonderfully made; your works are wonderful; I know that full well.

Reflection: Remember that you are made in the image of God. Your skin, your hair, your voice – everything that makes you YOU – is divinely designed. Celebrate your identity today and always.

____

____

____

____

____

____

____

____

____

____

____

____

____

____

____

Embrace Your Divine Journey

Reflections

5 Minute Blessing Journal

__/__/___

S M T W TH F S

Breathe before writing

How God blessed me today:

3 blessings I received today:

Today's Highlight

What song is in your heart?

Things that I learned today

Today's Scripture

Embrace Your Divine Journey

Strength and Resilience

Isaiah 40:31 - But those who hope in the Lord will renew their strength. They will soar on wings like eagles; they will run and not grow weary, they will walk and not faint.

Reflection: Think of all the times you've stood tall amidst adversity. God grants you the strength to overcome any obstacle. Rely on Him to continue guiding you through every challenge.

____

____

____

____

____

____

____

____

____

____

____

____

____

____

Reflections

Embrace Your Divine Journey

5 Minute Blessing Journal

__/__/___

S M T W TH F S

Breathe before writing

INHALE EXHALE INHALE EXHALE INHALE EXHALE

How God blessed me today:

What song is in your heart?

3 blessings I received today:

Today's Highlight

Things that I learned today

Today's Scripture

Self-Worth

Proverbs 31:10 - A wife of noble character who can find? She is worth far more than rubies.

Reflection: Remember your value isn't based on society's standards, but on the priceless love of the The Lord. You are cherished beyond measure.

____

____

____

____

____

____

____

____

____

____

____

____

____

____

____

Reflections

Rising in Radiance

5 Minute Blessing Journal

__/__/___

S M T W TH F S

Breathe before writing

INHALE EXHALE INHALE EXHALE INHALE EXHALE

How God blessed me today:

3 blessings I received today:

Today's Highlight

What song is in your heart?

Things that I learned today

Today's Scripture

Community

Hebrews 10:24-25 - And let us consider how we may spur one another on toward love and good deeds, not giving up meeting together, as some are in the habit of doing, but encouraging one another...

Reflection: Consider the power of sisterhood and community. Celebrate the bonds of love and unity with your fellow sisters.

Reflections

---

5 Minute Blessing Journal

__/__/___

S M T W TH F S

Breathe before writing

INHALE EXHALE INHALE EXHALE INHALE EXHALE

3 blessings I received today:

How God blessed me today:

Today's Highlight

What song is in your heart?

Things that I learned today

Today's Scripture

Faith Over Fear
2 Timothy 1:7 - For God has not given us a spirit of fear, but of power and of love and of a sound mind.

Reflection: As you navigate the world, remember that fear doesn't define you. God has given you power, love, and clarity. Trust in Him.

Embrace Your Divine Journey

Reflections

5 Minute Blessing Journal

__/__/___

S M T W TH F S

Breathe before writing

INHALE EXHALE INHALE EXHALE INHALE EXHALE

How God blessed me today:

3 blessings I received today:

Today's Highlight

What song is in your heart?

Things that I learned today

Today's Scripture

Embrace Your Divine Journey

Joy
Nehemiah 8:10 - The joy of the Lord is your strength.

Reflection: Find happiness in the Lord's presence. Embrace the joy that bubbles up from within, knowing it's a gift from Him.

Reflections

Embrace Your Divine Journey

5 Minute Blessing Journal

__ / __ / ___

S M T W TH F S

Breathe before writing

How God blessed me today:

____
____
____
____
____

What song is in your heart?

3 blessings I received today:

Today's Highlight

Things that I learned today

____
____
____
____

Today's Scripture

____
____

Ancestry and Heritage

Proverbs 13:22 - A good person leaves an inheritance for their children's children...

Reflection: Reflect on the legacy of your ancestors. Their strength, wisdom, and sacrifices have paved the way for you. Honor them in your prayers.

____

____

____

____

____

____

____

____

____

____

____

____

____

____

____

____

Embrace Your Divine Journey

Reflections

5 Minute Blessing Journal

__/__/___

S M T W TH F S

Breathe before writing

How God blessed me today:

3 blessings I received today:

Today's Highlight

What song is in your heart?

Things that I learned today

Today's Scripture

Embrace Your Divine Journey

Healing

Psalm 147:3 - He heals the brokenhearted and binds up their wounds.

Reflection: Whatever pain or trauma you're holding, surrender it to God. Trust in His capacity to heal and restore you.

____

____

____

____

____

____

____

____

____

____

____

____

____

____

____

Reflections

Embrace Your Divine Journey

5 Minute Blessing Journal

__ / __ / ___

S M T W TH F S

Breathe before writing

INHALE EXHALE INHALE EXHALE INHALE EXHALE

3 blessings I received today:

How God blessed me today:

Today's Highlight

What song is in your heart?

Things that I learned today

Today's Scripture

Confidence

Philippians 4:13 - I can do all things through Christ who strengthens me.

Reflection: Let go of doubts. You're equipped with divine power. Tackle any challenge with confidence, knowing God is by your side.

____

____

____

____

____

____

____

____

____

____

____

____

____

____

____

Reflections

5 Minute Blessing Journal

__/__/___

S M T W TH F S

Breathe before writing

INHALE EXHALE INHALE EXHALE INHALE EXHALE

How God blessed me today:

What song is in your heart?

Today's Scripture

3 blessings I received today:

Today's Highlight

Things that I learned today

Embrace Your Divine Journey

Wisdom

James 1:5 - If any of you lacks wisdom, you should ask God, who gives generously to all without finding fault, and it will be given to you.

Reflection: Seek divine guidance. As you make decisions, turn to God for wisdom and insight.

Reflections

5 Minute Blessing Journal

__/__/___

S M T W TH F S

Breathe before writing

INHALE EXHALE INHALE EXHALE INHALE EXHALE

3 blessings I received today:

How God blessed me today:

Today's Highlight

What song is in your heart?

Things that I learned today

Today's Scripture

Overcoming Challenges

Romans 8:28 - And we know that in all things God works for the good of those who love him, who have been called according to his purpose.

Reflection: Every trial has a purpose. Embrace challenges as opportunities for growth. God is orchestrating everything for your ultimate good.

Reflections

Rising in Radiance

5 Minute Blessing Journal

__/__/___

S M T W TH F S

Breathe before writing

INHALE EXHALE INHALE EXHALE INHALE EXHALE

How God blessed me today:

3 blessings I received today:

Today's Highlight

What song is in your heart?

Things that I learned today

Today's Scripture

Embrace Your Divine Journey

Self-Care

Mark 6:31 - Then, because so many people were coming and going that they did not even have a chance to eat, he said to them, 'Come with me by yourselves to a quiet place and get some rest.'

Reflection: Prioritize self-care. Rest, rejuvenation, and self-love are divine mandates. Treat yourself with the care and attention God desires for you.

Reflections

5 Minute Blessing Journal

__/__/___

S M T W TH F S

Breathe before writing

How God blessed me today:

3 blessings I received today:

What song is in your heart?

Today's Highlight

Things that I learned today

Today's Scripture

Rising in Radiance

Courage

Joshua 1:9 - Have I not commanded you? Be strong and courageous. Do not be afraid; do not be discouraged, for the Lord your God will be with you wherever you go.

Reflection: Step out with courage. Whatever you face, God's promise stands: He is with you, backing you up in every venture and challenge.

Embrace Your Divine Journey

Reflections

5 Minute Blessing Journal

__/__/___

S M T W TH F S

Breathe before writing

How God blessed me today:

3 blessings I received today:

What song is in your heart?

Today's Highlight

Things that I learned today

Today's Scripture

Embrace Your Divine Journey

Purpose and Destiny

Jeremiah 29:11 - For I know the plans I have for you, declares the Lord, plans to prosper you and not to harm you, plans to give you hope and a future.

Reflection: You are destined for greatness. God has mapped out an extraordinary journey for you. Trust in His plans and walk in your purpose.

____

____

____

____

____

____

____

____

____

____

____

____

____

____

____

Reflections

5 Minute Blessing Journal

__/__/___

S M T W TH F S

Breathe before writing

How God blessed me today:

____
____
____
____
____

What song is in your heart?

3 blessings I received today:

Today's Highlight

Things that I learned today

____
____
____
____

Today's Scripture

____
____

Beauty

Song of Solomon 4:7 - You are altogether beautiful, my darling; there is no flaw in you.

Reflection: Embrace your divine beauty, both inside and out. You are the epitome of God's artistry, and there's no flaw in His masterpiece.

Reflections

5 Minute Blessing Journal

__/__/___

S M T W TH F S

Breathe before writing

How God blessed me today:

What song is in your heart?

3 blessings I received today:

Today's Highlight

Things that I learned today

Today's Scripture

Embrace Your Divine Journey

Gratitude

I Thessalonians 5:18 - Give thanks in all circumstances; for this is God's will for you in Christ Jesus.

Reflection: Adopt an attitude of gratitude. Even in challenging times, find reasons to be thankful. Blessings surround you.

Reflections

Embrace Your Divine Journey

5 Minute Blessing Journal

__/__/___

S M T W TH F S

Breathe before writing

How God blessed me today:

What song is in your heart?

3 blessings I received today:

Today's Highlight

Things that I learned today

Today's Scripture

Liberation

Galatians 5:1 - It is for freedom that Christ has set us free. Stand firm, then, and do not let yourselves be burdened again by a yoke of slavery.

Reflection: God desires your freedom. Whether it's societal chains or internal battles, stand firm in the freedom Christ offers.

Reflections

5 Minute Blessing Journal

__/__/___

S M T W TH F S

Breathe before writing

INHALE EXHALE INHALE EXHALE INHALE EXHALE

How God blessed me today:

3 blessings I received today:

Today's Highlight

What song is in your heart?

Things that I learned today

Today's Scripture

Embrace Your Divine Journey

Growth and Transformation

II Corinthians 5:17 - Therefore, if anyone is in Christ, the new creation has come: The old has gone, the new is here!

Reflection: Celebrate your evolution. With every prayer, every act of faith, you are growing and transforming into the best version of yourself.

Reflections

Embrace Your Divine Journey

5 Minute Blessing Journal

__ / __ / ___

S M T W TH F S

Breathe before writing

INHALE EXHALE INHALE EXHALE INHALE EXHALE

How God blessed me today:

What song is in your heart?

Today's Scripture

3 blessings I received today:

Today's Highlight

Things that I learned today

Sisterhood

Proverbs 27:17 - As iron sharpens iron, so one person sharpens another.

Reflection: Cherish the bond with your sisters. They are your allies, your confidantes, your iron. Together, you become stronger.

____

____

____

____

____

____

____

____

____

____

____

____

____

____

____

Reflections

5 Minute Blessing Journal

__/__/___

S M T W TH F S

Breathe before writing

INHALE EXHALE INHALE EXHALE INHALE EXHALE

How God blessed me today:

What song is in your heart?

Today's Scripture

3 blessings I received today:

Today's Highlight

Things that I learned today

Embrace Your Divine Journey

Divine Protection

Psalm 91:11 - For he will command his angels concerning you to guard you in all your ways.

Reflection: Rest assured in God's protection. His angels are always around you, shielding you from harm.

____

____

____

____

____

____

____

____

____

____

____

____

____

____

____

____

Reflections

Embrace Your Divine Journey

5 Minute Blessing Journal

__/__/___

S M T W TH F S

Breathe before writing

How God blessed me today:

What song is in your heart?

3 blessings I received today:

Today's Highlight

Things that I learned today

Today's Scripture

Authenticity

Psalm 51:6 - Behold, you desire truth in the innermost being, and in the hidden part you will make me know wisdom.

Reflection: Be unapologetically you. God desires your genuine self. Embrace your authenticity, knowing it's in truth that you truly shine.

Reflections

Rising in Radiance

5 Minute Blessing Journal

__/__/___

S M T W TH F S

Breathe before writing

3 blessings I received today:

How God blessed me today:

Today's Highlight

What song is in your heart?

Things that I learned today

Today's Scripture

Embrace Your Divine Journey

Faithfulness

Lamentations 3:22-23 - The steadfast love of the Lord never ceases; his mercies never come to an end; they are new every morning; great is your faithfulness.

Reflection: Relish in God's unfailing love and faithfulness. His commitment to you is unwavering, and every dawn brings fresh mercies tailored just for you.

Reflections

Embrace Your Divine Journey

5 Minute Blessing Journal

__ / __ / ___

S M T W TH F S

Breathe before writing

How God blessed me today:

____
____
____
____
____

What song is in your heart?

3 blessings I received today:

Today's Highlight

Things that I learned today

____
____
____
____

Today's Scripture

____
____

Victory

I Corinthians 15:57 - But thanks be to God! He gives us the victory through our Lord Jesus Christ.

Reflection: Celebrate your wins, both big and small. Every achievement is a testament to God's favor and power in your life. You are destined for victory!

____

____

____

____

____

____

____

____

____

____

____

____

____

____

____

Embrace Your Divine Journey

Reflections

5 Minute Blessing Journal

__/__/___

S M T W TH F S

Breathe before writing

INHALE EXHALE INHALE EXHALE INHALE EXHALE

How God blessed me today:

3 blessings I received today:

Today's Highlight

What song is in your heart?

Things that I learned today

Today's Scripture

Embrace Your Divine Journey

Boundless Love

Romans 8:38-39 - For I am convinced that neither death nor life, neither angels nor demons, neither the present nor the future, nor any powers, neither height nor depth, nor anything else in all creation, will be able to separate us from the love of God that is in Christ Jesus our Lord.

Reflection: Embrace the infinite love God has for you. There's no force in the universe that can break that bond. You are eternally cherished.

Reflections

Embrace Your Divine Journey

5 Minute Blessing Journal

__ / __ / ___

S M T W TH F S

Breathe before writing

How God blessed me today:

3 blessings I received today:

Today's Highlight

What song is in your heart?

Things that I learned today

Today's Scripture

Abundance

John 10:10 - The thief comes only to steal and kill and destroy; I have come that they may have life and have it to the full.

Reflection: God desires abundance for you, not just in material blessings but in joy, love, peace, and every good thing. Claim your abundant life.

____

____

____

____

____

____

____

____

____

____

____

____

____

____

Reflections

5 Minute Blessing Journal

__/__/___

S M T W TH F S

Breathe before writing

How God blessed me today:

What song is in your heart?

Today's Scripture

3 blessings I received today:

Today's Highlight

Things that I learned today

Embrace Your Divine Journey

Legacy

Proverbs 13:22 - A good person leaves an inheritance for their children's children.

Reflection: Reflect on the legacy you are building. Your actions today have the power to influence generations. Lead with love, wisdom, and intention.

____

____

____

____

____

____

____

____

____

____

____

____

____

____

____

Reflections

Embrace Your Divine Journey

5 Minute Blessing Journal

__ / __ / ___

S M T W TH F S

Breathe before writing

INHALE EXHALE INHALE EXHALE INHALE EXHALE

3 blessings I received today:

How God blessed me today:

Today's Highlight

What song is in your heart?

Things that I learned today

Today's Scripture

Trust

Proverbs 3:5-6 - Trust in the Lord with all your heart and lean not on your own understanding; in all your ways submit to him, and he will make your paths straight.

Reflection: Entrust your journey to God. Even when the road is unclear, His divine GPS never fails. He's guiding you to your destined place.

Reflections

5 Minute Blessing Journal

__/__/___

S M T W TH F S

Breathe before writing

How God blessed me today:

What song is in your heart?

3 blessings I received today:

Today's Highlight

Things that I learned today

Today's Scripture

Embrace Your Divine Journey

Grace

II Corinthians 12:9 - But he said to me, 'My grace is sufficient for you, for my power is made perfect in weakness.' Therefore, I will boast all the more gladly about my weaknesses, so that Christ's power may rest on me.

Reflection: Revel in God's grace. It's the gentle cushion in your moments of weakness, lifting you and highlighting His power in your life.

____

____

____

____

____

____

____

____

____

____

____

____

____

Reflections

5 Minute Blessing Journal

__/__/___

S M T W TH F S

Breathe before writing

INHALE EXHALE INHALE EXHALE INHALE EXHALE

3 blessings I received today:

How God blessed me today:

Today's Highlight

What song is in your heart?

Things that I learned today

Today's Scripture

Boldness

Hebrews 4:16 - Let us then approach God's throne of grace with confidence, so that we may receive mercy and find grace to help us in our time of need.

Reflection: Step boldly in your faith journey. God has granted you direct access to His throne. Approach Him with confidence, knowing He's eager to listen.

____

____

____

____

____

____

____

____

____

____

____

____

____

____

____

____

Reflections

5 Minute Blessing Journal

__/__/___

S M T W TH F S

Breathe before writing

3 blessings I received today:

How God blessed me today:

Today's Highlight

What song is in your heart?

Things that I learned today

Today's Scripture

Embrace Your Divine Journey

Celebration

Psalm 118:24 - This is the day the Lord has made; let us rejoice and be glad in it.

Reflection: Celebrate the gift of life and the journey you've undertaken these past 30 days. Every day is a divine gift filled with purpose. Rejoice in the present, eager for the future God has for you.

Reflections

Embrace Your Divine Journey

__/__/___

S M T W TH F S

Breathe before writing

How God blessed me today:

What song is in your heart?

3 blessings I received today:

Today's Highlight

Things that I learned today

Today's Scripture

"...Therefore if the Son makes you free, you shall be free indeed." John 8:36

Reflect on a moment when you truly felt like a queen. How does that moment connect to your spiritual journey?

____

____

____

____

____

____

____

____

____

____

____

____

____

____

____

____

____

____

____

____

Think of a piece of wisdom passed down from the women in your family. How has it fortified your faith?

Embrace Your Divine Journey

Describe a time when your resilience surprised you.
How can prayer further empower this innate strength?

____

____

____

____

____

____

____

____

____

____

____

____

____

____

____

____

____

____

____

How do you see the beauty of your skin intertwined with your spiritual journey?

Celebrate a fellow black woman who has uplifted you.
How has she inspired your spiritual growth?

____

____

____

____

____

____

____

____

____

____

____

____

____

____

____

____

____

____

____

____

Think of a gospel song or hymn that moves your soul.
What memories or feelings does it evoke, and why?

Reflect on your proudest achievement. How did faith play a role in reaching that pinnacle?

Write about a dream you're nurturing. How can daily prayer help it flourish?

____

____

____

____

____

____

____

____

____

____

____

____

____

____

____

____

____

____

____

____

Explore how your cultural heritage enriches your connection to God.

____

____

____

____

____

____

____

____

____

____

____

____

____

____

____

____

____

____

Recall a challenge where you felt God's grace guiding you. What did that moment teach you?

____

____

____

____

____

____

____

____

____

____

____

____

____

____

____

____

____

____

____

Embrace Your Divine Journey

Imagine a future where your faith plays a pivotal role. What does that world look like?

____

____

____

____

____

____

____

____

____

____

____

____

____

____

____

____

____

____

Dive deep into the spiritual significance and memories attached to your hair journey.

____

____

____

____

____

____

____

____

____

____

____

____

____

____

____

____

____

____

____

____

Envision the next level in your spiritual journey. What steps will take you there?

Describe a time when your boldness was a testament to your faith. How did it impact those around you?

____

____

____

____

____

____

____

____

____

____

____

____

____

____

____

____

____

____

____

____

Which scripture provides you with unparalleled comfort? Dive into its significance in your life.

Rising in Radiance

Explore how your personal style is an expression of your faith and identity.

____

____

____

____

____

____

____

____

____

____

____

____

____

____

____

____

____

____

____

Embrace Your Divine Journey

Ponder the spiritual legacy you aim to leave for the next generation of black women.

How does music enhance your prayer life, and which artists/songs resonate most?

____

____

____

____

____

____

____

____

____

____

____

____

____

____

____

____

____

____

____

____

Embrace Your Divine Journey

Dive into the divine feminine energy within you. How does it manifest in your day-to-day life?

Describe your ideal space for prayer and reflection. What makes it spiritually significant?

____

____

____

____

____

____

____

____

____

____

____

____

____

____

____

____

____

____

____

Reflect on the intersection of your life's purpose and your faith. How do they enrich one another?

Recall a joyous occasion where you felt God's presence.
Celebrate that memory and its lessons.

____

____

____

____

____

____

____

____

____

____

____

____

____

____

____

____

____

____

____

____

Embrace Your Divine Journey

List out blessings that have a special place in your heart. Reflect on their significance.

Just as seasons change, so does our spiritual journey. Which 'season' are you in now, and what is its essence?

____

____

____

____

____

____

____

____

____

____

____

____

____

____

____

____

____

____

____

Reflect on a moment in nature that deepened your connection with God.

How does your faith influence your style, and how do you express your spirituality through fashion?

Embrace Your Divine Journey

Think of a lesson learned the hard way. How has it illuminated your path?

Explore the spiritual side of self-care. How do you nurture your soul?

Embrace Your Divine Journey

Think about the rhythms and dances that connect you to your roots and spirituality. How do they move you?

____

____

____

____

____

____

____

____

____

____

____

____

____

____

____

____

____

____

____

Reflect on a time of healing, be it physical, spiritual, or emotional. How did your faith aid this process?

____

____

____

____

____

____

____

____

____

____

____

____

____

____

____

____

____

____

____

"…being confident of this, that he who began a good work in you will carry it on to completion until the day of Christ Jesus." Philippians 1:6

What has God done for you since you started this
journey?

What has God revealed to you since you started this journey?

Congratulations, radiant one!

You've turned the final page of this journal, but let's pause and recognize it for what it truly is — not an end, but a monumental landmark in your ongoing journey. *Rising in Radiance* has been your silent confidant, a sacred space where your soul's whispers and heart's cries have intertwined with ink, crafting a legacy of resilience, faith, and unabashed hope.

Now, stand still for a moment. Breathe in the magnitude of what you've accomplished. These pages cradled more than mere words; they've held your fears, your joys, your prayers, and your most intimate reflections. They've witnessed a narrative of transformation that's uniquely yours, a tale of a woman who, with each passing day, has unfolded into the most authentic version of herself.

But dear heart, reflection doesn't conclude here. It's a lifelong dialogue, an eternal dance between your earthly steps and your spiritual ambitions. Look back on these pages — your penned journey — not with finality but with a celebratory spirit, acknowledging your growth, your strength, and the incredible depth of your inner being.

Your completed prompts are keys to unlocking a treasure of insights. Reflection is not just an act of reminiscence; it's an empowering proclamation that every challenge faced, every prayer whispered, every tear shed, and every smile shared, has woven the fabric of your radiant present.

As you move forward, let this journal be a testament to your courage, a reminder that you're capable of facing the unknown, armed with faith, grace, and an indomitable spirit. Let it be a beacon, illuminating your path as you continue to rise, to thrive, to dazzle.

So, here's to you, beloved! Here's to the tears that watered your soul's garden, to the laughter that painted rainbows in your skies, to the prayers that moved mountains in your heart. You embarked on a journey of a thousand spiritual miles, and you've traversed in grace, in faith, in radiance.

As you close this journal, remember this isn't the end but a luminous beginning. You've delved into 30 days of profound reflections, immersing yourself in a way that reaffirms your divine identity and purpose. But the journey doesn't end here. Let the revelations you've uncovered be the wings upon which you soar, and the foundation upon which you stand tall. In a world that sometimes whispers doubts, let this journal remind you of your radiant worth and divine connection.

Every step, every reflection in this journey is a testament to your strength, faith, and divine purpose. Walk with confidence and conviction, backed by the

Rising in Radiance

unwavering love and power of God. Your journey is filled with promise, purpose, and an abundance of blessings. Radiate, dear sister, for the world awaits your light.

Continue to meditate on these words and scriptures, drawing strength, inspiration, and confidence from them. Embrace your journey with unwavering faith, knowing that you are divinely guided and profoundly loved. Every day is a step closer to the destiny God has crafted just for you. Take a moment to look back at the list of what you were believing in God for as you began this journey, how many ways has He moved in your life? What scriptures will you stand on to remain confident and encouraged? Use the following pages to pen your thoughts and reflect of God's goodness and grace.

Go forth, dear sister, with unwavering confidence and boundless faith. The world awaits the powerful testimony of your spirit. Stand tall, shine bright, and let every day be a testament to your divine journey. Embrace your legacy. Live your faith. *Rise in Radiance*.

Reflections

Reflections

Embrace Your Divine Journey

Reflections

Rising in Radiance

Reflections

Embrace Your Divine Journey

Reflections

Reflections

Embrace Your Divine Journey

Reflections

Reflections

Embrace Your Divine Journey

Reflections

Reflections

Reflections

Reflections

Embrace Your Divine Journey

Rising in Radiance

Discover the essence of empowerment with MeEvolv Devotionals, Journals & Planners, specially crafted for women of color. Our collection resonates with the unique journeys, dreams, and aspirations of every vibrant woman out there. MeEvolv Devotionals, Journals and Planners are crafted with precision and passion, our collection is designed to guide you through every step of your evolution. Whether you're setting goals, tracking progress, or simply seeking clarity, MeEvolv is your companion in the quest for a better you. Dive deep into self-reflection, plan your days with purpose, and watch yourself evolve. Continue your journey with MeEvolv today.

Visit www.MeEvolv.com for a full list of our products.

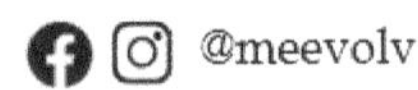

Embrace Your Divine Journey